THINGS TH[...]

ON THE LAND

A Crabtree Roots Book

CHRISTINA EARLEY

CRABTREE
Publishing Company
www.crabtreebooks.com

T0012387

School-to-Home Support for Caregivers and Teachers

This book helps children grow by letting them practice reading. Here are a few guiding questions to help the reader with building his or her comprehension skills. Possible answers appear here in red.

Before Reading:

- What do I think this book is about?
  - *I think this book is about vehicles that are driven on the land.*
  - *I think this book is about types of things that move on land.*

- What do I want to learn about this topic?
  - *I want to learn what kinds of vehicles drive on the land.*
  - *I want to learn about different types of things that move on land.*

During Reading:

- I wonder why...
  - *I wonder why snowmobiles can go on the snow.*
  - *I wonder why land vehicles are different from road vehicles.*

- What have I learned so far?
  - *I have learned that dune buggies go on sand.*
  - *I have learned that golf carts are driven on golf courses.*

After Reading:

- What details did I learn about this topic?
  - *I have learned there are different types of vehicles that move on land.*
  - *I have learned that people have special vehicles to help them move on land.*

- Read the book again and look for the vocabulary words.
  - *I see the words **dune buggy** on page 4 and the word **snowmobiles** on page 10. The other vocabulary words are found on page 14.*

How many **vehicles** do you see on the land?

One **dune buggy**.

Two **tractors**.

Three **golf carts**.

Four **snowmobiles**.

People use vehicles on the land.

Word List

Sight Words

do	on	three
four	one	two
how	see	use
many	the	you

Words to Know

dune buggy

golf carts

snowmobiles

tractors

vehicles

25 Words

How many **vehicles** do you see on the land?

One **dune buggy**.

Two **tractors**.

Three **golf carts**.

Four **snowmobiles**.

People use vehicles on the land.

THINGS THAT GO ON THE LAND

Written by: Christina Earley
Designed by: Rhea Wallace
Series Development: James Earley
Proofreader: Melissa Boyce
Educational Consultant: Marie Lemke M.Ed.
Photographs:
Shutterstock: Valentin Valkov.: cover, p. 1; Artie
    Medvedev: p. 3, 14; pixinoo: p. 5, 14; Emjay Smith:
    p. 6-7, 14; sirtravelalot: p. 8, 14; Olhna Pashkovska:
    p. 10, 14; novak.elcic: p. 12

Library and Archives Canada Cataloguing in Publication

Available at the Library and Archives Canada

Library of Congress Cataloging-in-Publication Data

Available at the Library of Congress

Crabtree Publishing Company

www.crabtreebooks.com   1-800-387-7650

Printed in the U.S.A./062021/CG20210401

Published in the United States
Crabtree Publishing
347 Fifth Avenue, Suite 1402-145
New York, NY, 10016

Published in Canada
Crabtree Publishing
616 Welland Ave.
St. Catharines, Ontario L2M 5V6